Narrative Therapy

Life Story and Tree Of Life For Trauma

This Book Belongs To

Tree Of Life

Storms - (Challenges)

Leave - (Significant people)

Fruit - (Gifts)

Trunk - (Skills)

Roots - (Where I came From)

Ground - (Present Life)

Branches - (Dreams)

Tree Of Life

Storms - (Challenges)

Leave - (Significant people)

Fruit - (Gifts)

Trunk - (Skills)

Roots - (Where I came From)

Ground - (Present Life)

Branches - (Dreams)

Notes

Notes

My Life Story

MY PAST

What is the story of my past?

What challenges have I had to overcome?

What strengths have I gained form my past experiences?

Notes

Notes

My Life Story

MY PRESENT

How would I describe my present life and type of person that I am?

Am I different from the person I was in my past?

Am I currently facing any new challenges?

Notes

Notes

My Life Story

MY FUTURE

What does my ideal future look like?

Would it be different to how it is now, If so how?

Who is in my future?

Notes

Notes

Reflection Question

STORMS - (Challenges)

- Storms might include- mental health problems, friends or family conflict and/or lack of resources and support.
- What storms have you experienced in the past?
- What obstacles do you need to overcome?
- What storms might you experience in the future?

LEAVE - (SIGNIFICANT PEOPLE)

- Who plays an important role in your life?
- Who are the people that your trust and turn to for support?
- What makes you trust them?
- How have they influenced your life so far?
- Do they know they are important to you?

FRUIT - (GIFTS)

- What compliments have you received?
- What are some of your strengths?
- Have the significant people in your life helped shape your strengths?
- Have you ever received any materialistic gifts that have helped you?
- What strength are you working on at the moment?

TRUNK - (SKILLS)

- What are your top 3 skills?
- How did you develop your coping skills and abilities?
- Did anything impact your coping skills?
- Do you focus more on your faults, rather than your skills?

Notes

Notes

Reflection Question

ROOTS - (WHERE I CAME FROM)

- Where were you born?
- What are your favorite memories ?
- Who helped shape your life ?
- Do you think your past has influenced your present life?

GROUND - (PRESENT LIFE)

- What is the best thing about your present life?
- How do you like to spend your spare time?
- What do you wish you had more time for?
- What do you value the most?

BRANCES - (DREAMS)

- If you had three wishes, what would they be?
- Would you use your wishes to better yourself?
- Would you give any of your wishes to other people ? If so, who and why?

Notes

Notes

Check In

How Are You Feeling?

BREATHE	Take 5 deep breathes in and Centre yourself.
FEEL	Check in with your body and mind. How are you feeling today?
THANK	Name 3 things you are grateful for?
AFFIRM	Take a moment to say 5 nice things that yo like about yourself.
NEED	What do you need in order to make yourself feel better?

Notes

Notes

CHALLENGING NEGATIVE THOUGHTS

AM I MAKING ASSUMPTIONS?

IS THERE ANOTHER WAY TO LOOK AT IT?

WHAT ARE OTHER POSSIBLE OUTCOMES?

IS THERE EVIDENCE FOR THIS WORRY?

WHAT ADVICE WOULD I GIVE TO A FRIEND?

IS THIS WORRY IN OR OUT OF MY CONTROL?

Notes

Notes

Imagine you are holding a flower

Breathe slowly in through your
nose and smell the fresh air

Breathe out slowly through your
mouth and watch the petals fly
off the flower

Notes

Notes

Close your eyes and imagine you

are holding a feather

Breathe in slowly and fill your

belly with as much air as you

can

Blow out slowly through your

mouth and watch the feather

float away

Notes

Notes

Notes

www.ingramcontent.com/pod-product-compliance
Lightning Source LLC
LaVergne TN
LVHW060045210926
848481LV00013B/3962